rip tides

NADIA STARBINSKI

RIP TIDES

NADIA STARBINSKI

to those who inspired it and will not read it

RIP TIDES

ACKNOWLEDGEMENTS

I never understood the impact of my words until I was praised for a craft I never acknowledged. I've spent countless hours of countless days questioning myself and where my journey was supposed to take me. I spent more time trying to determine the outcome than I did experiencing the lessons that brought me there in the first place. I have made many mistakes. I have cried many tears. And I have met many amazing souls that I will carry in my heart for lifetimes.

It's not about where you go or how you get there, it is about the story you will tell.

Thank you for listening to mine.

RIP TIDES

I.
three sheets to the wind
advice your drunk mother gave you

RIP TIDES

May your souls find peace through the bridge of my words.
May your bleeding hearts find a voice of sanctity.
May you carry on.

Kick the toxic from your life.
It is hard to part ways with your comfort zone,
but the way you'll blossom from it
will build a garden that'll take your breath away.

You can tell the direction you're going in with someone by the
way they say your name.
Next time you speak with someone, anyone,
listen for the genuineness
of their intentions.

I've learned
you cannot force somebody
to realize your worth
and even if you could,
you shouldn't have to.

NADIA STARBINSKI

You cannot immerse yourself completely
into a person
and not expect to drown.

Delete his number
so that on nights
when eight shots still don't taste like enough
to stop the aching
and your blood turns to liquor
and you let the alcohol
fill your lungs until you choke,

you won't call him to save you... because he's not going to
come.

And when he sends you straight to voicemail,
you won't want to be saved anyway.

You were created to make someone else's life better.
Somebody needs what you have.

God did not give you the strength to stand up so you can run back to the thing that knocked you down.

This emptiness gets haunting sometimes, no doubt.
And sometimes it's hard to keep your head above water.
Sometimes waves of emotion become overwhelming and some
nights you'll feel like drowning,
but the hardest part is to admit when you're lost.

I am lost.

I will never understand
how or why the things in our life
happen the way that they do,
and I don't think we're supposed to.
But I do know that all those things happen
just as they are meant to.
We are placed in the situations we are in because
God knows we can overcome them,
and that they will only make us stronger.
We are brought into people's lives because we are meant to
learn a lesson (or teach one).

Every soul we've crossed,
every obstacle we've jumped,
everything we've touched,
or has touched us,
has made us who we are
in this very moment.

Be blessed by your losses but be made whole with what can be built from the rubble.

People are placed in our lives,
whether it for a lifetime
or for a season,
and we must accept this as fact.
They show us a side of ourselves we've dismissed.
They bring us to the well and tell us to drink.

They walk us through a new stage and once we get there...we
must part ways.

I've learned not to question this journey. I've learned to enjoy
it and take it as is.

Sometimes the heartbreak itself is the purpose,
Sometimes the timing is the purpose.
Sometimes not knowing is the purpose.

Love may be like heaven,
But it hurts like hell.

Growth isn't always comforting,
but it is always necessary.

Pray to God, even after He gave you what you were praying for.

Don't be eye candy,
be soul food.

If you hold on
to certain things
from your past,
that just means
you believe
they still serve you
in a good way.

NADIA STARBINSKI

Be careful who you invite into your soul.

If a person wants to be a part of your life, they will make an obvious effort to do so.

Pay attention to people's timing.

Think twice before reserving a space in your heart for people who only stay when it's convenient or beneficial for them.

Produce joy.

Always drive
with your windows down on a nice day.
And always sing along,
even if you don't know the words.

It is so easy to get lost in the negativity of this world.
Be the light at the end of someone's tunnel.

Be kind to each other, always.

You don't need to be perfect to inspire others.
Let people get inspired by how you deal with your
imperfection.

Yes, fear is hard to overcome, but missing out on all of life's best moments is more terrifying than trying them out

1. you cannot keep water dead flowers.

The friendships and relationships you have now fit a specific timeline. Some last a lifetime, some last only a season. While each relationship is unique to aiding your growth, you cannot force someone to overstay his or her welcome; it becomes toxic to you and the continuation to your journey. People come into your life and they serve their purpose by bringing you to a specific place – the place you're supposed to be at – and then they no longer do anything. They become an anchor holding you down to one spot and you can't continue to grow when you have roots holding you to a place where there is no sunlight.

2. the choices you make don't define you, but they definitely leave an impact.

Growing up forces you to make difficult decisions – something you've probably heard your entire life. Some decisions may be simpler than others, however, each one is responsible for the outcome that later forms the character of who you are today. These decisions aid in molding you, they do not define you. You will look back in ten years and realize how your choices, good or bad, created the successful person in the mirror.

3. it's okay to be selfish.

I've spent too much of my time catering to others. I've always put others before myself, whether it is emotionally or physically. Sometimes it's okay to say no to something. It's okay to reject someone. It's okay to put yourself first and do something that pleases you despite popular opinion. This leads me to my next point:

4. choose yourself.

Cliché right? "Make yourself a priority." "You can't love until you learn to love yourself." "Do what makes you happy" ... blah blah blah. But let's for one-second step out of our comfort zones and this banal definition of self-acceptance and look a little deeper. We've become these robotic young adults who are so afraid to show emotion other than happiness in fear that our feelings aren't validated or don't benefit our growth.
We can be brave without being selfish, and we can be happy without the bullshit.

5. try.

This was my hardest lesson and most important to learn. It is easy to get caught up in life and forget about your priorities. It is easier at 18 years old to refuse your potential and fall into patterns of the bare minimum. Life is hard. You should never forget where your skills lie and where your capabilities can take you.

never give up, despite the obstacles that will deter you.

It's easy not to fail
when you're not trying
to do anything
great.

Grow out of meaningless relationships.

If they are not motivating your success, then they do not deserve to benefit from it.

NADIA STARBINSKI

The day you realize that everyone else's opinion means
nothing, you realize what you're meant to do with your life.

I refuse to put myself in the place I was before because it took so much to get out of it.

Your growth scares people who don't want to change.

God puts people in your life
for a reason,
and removes them from your life
for a better reason.

Pay attention to who reached out to you in times of need.

I hope you make peace with your pain.

Some things just aren't worth stressing over.
Life goes on.

There's so much to live for and I hope that nobody ever loses sight of that.

NADIA STARBINSKI

Do everything with a good heart and expect nothing in return.
You will never be disappointed.

I think that when you have a connection with someone it never really goes away.

I pray we're right for each other.

Give yourself permission to realize there's a point to all of this.

It's amazing how liberated you feel when you stop giving attention to all the things that never reciprocated.

The best way to deal with someone that only wants you when it's convenient for them is to not deal with them at all.

It's funny how the people who demand respect are the same people who forget how to give it.

RIP TIDES

NADIA STARBINSKI

RIP TIDES

II.
deep six
disposed memories

RIP TIDES

It's 4:16 in the morning and the only thing I'm craving is you.

———

I can't quite grasp the concept of you not wanting me.

Everyone wants to romanticize sadness but there's nothing beautiful about getting caught up in your own head

-reality check

4:41am - Passive aggressive smiling because we both fucked up but can't admit it.

5:03am - I can't move on because it was supposed to be us and you thought different.

6:36am - The room was on fire and you were still thinking of her while I was thinking of us.

7:58am - Does she give you goose bumps? Does she make your skin crawl?

8:02am - It was supposed to be us.

9:00am - I love you please come back

9:29am - I stopped taking my coffee with sugar because it reminded me of your laugh

9:34am - I rolled over onto another boy this morning. I spent two nights with him and I think I fell in love.

9:57am - I left him there because I remembered the way you held me in the early hours of the morning and he just bite my neck and grabbed my waist.

10:13am - You were toxic, and I hate you for making my fingers bleed when I touched you.

10:40am - It was supposed to be us.

11:04am – I was walking into work and I had this flashback of us walking in the parking lot when you told me I made you whole. You said it so quietly under your breath, I wasn't sure I heard you right (even though you said it again when I looked back).

11:07am - You're the most beautiful skeleton in my closet.

11:11am - Make a wish.

12:09pm - I don't feel sad.

1:34pm - Then again, I don't feel anything.

2:02pm - Hopefulness came in a pretty package and my God, did I want to open it.

3:18pm - It was supposed to be us.

4:06pm - There's that saying that says it's better to have loved and lost than to have never loved at all. I never could fathom why anyone would choose to never love at all. It wasn't until you left me that I finally understood.

5:11pm - I wish I never loved you at all.

5:53pm - I'm stuck.

6:10pm - Walk through me. I don't exist.

6:26pm - It was supposed to be us.

7:09pm - I don't want to look back and see something broken, or something that was better off left unopened.

7:39pm - I hope she's gentle when she waters the flowers in your lungs and plants kisses on your forehead.

8:50pm - I remember how your lips tasted like lilacs.

9:32pm - I hate flowers.

10:19pm - You're the kind of guy people write poetry about.

10:49pm - I burned my tongue when I kissed you and I guess that should've been the first clue that this would go up in flames.

11:11pm - Make a wish.

11:46pm - It was supposed to be us.

12:00am - Theodore Roosevelt wrote in his diary the night his wife and mother passed, "X, the light has gone out of my life."

12:45am - I've never been told I was desirable with the lights on.

12:58am - It's getting late and you're not here.

1:00am - This new boy is covering me in kisses and each one makes me flinch because they're metallic and burns holes in my skin where yours wrapped me in silk.

2:10am - I don't know God, but when I'm sad I ask him to take me.

2:48am - There's a loneliness in this world so great that you can see it in the slow movement of the hands on a clock.

3:12am - Hold me and tell me I'm home.

3:30am - My head hurts.

3:46am - I don't think "home" has any meaning as a word anymore. I used to think it was in a person, but my home has switched so many times...I can write all I want about how it has been in your eyes for the last infinity and how I picked it over my sanity, but the truth is I don't know why I picked you. Trying to live in your heart felt like living somewhere I didn't belong.
4:01am- But I'd let you drag me to hell if it meant I got to hold your hand.

4:41am - It was supposed to be us.

- twenty-four hours of mourning

Maybe you meant it when you said you loved me, or maybe I reminded you of a good nights' rest or freshly brewed coffee and you were just homesick.

- you can't make homes out of people

He made me believe that stars smile, brighter than how they shine. But he also showed me that skies cry, louder than their own light.

- deception

Forgive me for the ashes. It seems that after years of pinning for suns and stars I have finally found my fire- dare you fan my flames?

- self-awareness

1. When I was a child, I believed that I could swallow a piece of the sun, a cherry blossom, or a bit of ocean water, and become beautiful. I did these things, but when I grew up the sun burned down what I had built, the blossom took root and crowded my lungs, and while they were beautiful...I couldn't breathe. The ocean water took out the fire but drowned what was left.

In other words, I couldn't let go of what people had done to me. I loved the sadness a little too much, and all that showed on the outside. Nobody ever thought me beautiful. The ugly ones like me are powerful but only when we learn to grow past it. Guess who still hasn't learned?

2. I remember a year ago I was dragging all the seas around me, like a saltwater ball and chain, and everybody else knew how to swim. I was kicking and gasping and struggling, until I wasn't. Until I was sitting in the corner half-dead, all blue, and then I somehow managed to drag myself to the surface, through the sand. I called it victory. Everybody else called it doing the bare minimum.

In other words, I didn't apply for very many scholarships. I had to take out a student loan. I panicked every hour of every day, and at night I couldn't sleep. At night I cried and contemplated doing things. Yes, this is what I'm always writing poetry about...I wish I could say it feels good to get the truth off my chest, but it doesn't.

3. In September I mistakenly believed I had become the moon. Full of craters, yes, only capable of reflecting other people's light, yes, but damn if I wasn't in control of all the oceans.

In other words, I thought everybody could forgive my mistake and we could move on. I thought I could apply myself this year and engage in things that would make everybody proud of me again.

4. I was wrong.

5. I paint to hide my face. I wish I could sweep the pigments and formulas like I do words, but I am not that talented. Maybe I don't even do the words thing right.

In other words, I learned to apply makeup for two reasons. The first was because I'm never enough and I'm tired of that. (See Verse 1) The second was because I started crying all the time, when I'm alone, and I don't want people to know.

6. My mother tells me I am still a child. I lock myself in my room and tell myself that I will grow. I am growing. I just have to move past wanting to stop existing, first.

- six stages of growing up

I am the woman you will never forget.

I am the spirit that will haunt your dreams
late night
as you turn to hold her,
your lover,
your placeholder.

I am the woman for whom your body aches
as you taste me
again
and again
on her lips,
The woman whose passion fills your senses
as you hear my voice
in every moan
she fakes.

I am the shadow that seizes your heart
each time you whisper,
"I love you,"
wishing
she were
me.

I am the feeling that paralyzes you
each time you see my ghost
in a cup of tea
on a rainy day,
on the smudge of dark lipstick on your pillow,
when unabashed laughter
fills the room,
or as the seasons change
and you remember
how I changed too.

I am the love that holds you

bound to yesterdays.
The love that forces you
to your knees.
I am the void
that weighs on your memory;
heavy,
breathing
and alive.

I will linger on in your mind
long after you've closed your eyes,

I am the question that drips off your tongue:
How could I have lost her?

But you know.

- the one that got away

It's been 209 days since I've said, "I love you," and heard it back.

I sit up at night writing poetry about how you've crushed my heart; how the air is salt, and my lungs are a big open wound. But I want to write beautiful words about an unabashed love so pure that cupid himself can't believe his eyes. I want to fill my journals with endless stories of two friends-turned- lovers who lived happily ever after.

And I've realized I can't until I move forward- and I mean really move forward.

It's been 209 days of some form of thought of you. I've tried to kiss boys just to wash the taste of you out of my mouth, but your touch lives forever on my skin no matter how many hours I've spent drowning myself in the bathtub. I've been turned upside down and I can't seem to get off this carousel.

A part of me is still in shock.
More-so of the idea that you can hold me in your arms, look me in the eyes and tell me I am your everything and in less than 12 hours, I am a ghost.
I was too busy trying to build up our sandcastle of a life while you were the tide that kept washing it away and I never quite understood why I wasn't good enough.

I was often so swiftly kicked to the back of the closet after I provided for you the attention you craved. The hurt that comes with the knowledge that I was only necessary to you for those few moments of pleasure is something I still struggle to shake.

I have experienced heartbreak, and I'm sure I'll experience it again.

But this time it was different; my entire world collapsed at my feet and I had no idea how to start over, but I did.

I rose from the ashes of our relationship and worked on me for the first time in a very long time - and I'm thankful for your part in that.
You were the big wrecking ball that had to come down on my comfort zone, and every day I am sad that it had to happen in order for my greatness to be revealed.

There are days where my body is tired, and I wish I had your arms. There are moments where I come across an old memory and I have to talk myself out of storing it in the back of my mind for later. There are nights I lie awake because I forgot how to sleep without the sound of your breathing.

You hurt me in the worst way a human heart can bleed.

But if you take anything out of this letter, it is that *I am happy*.

And I hope with everything in me that you are too.

- closure

I left our last kiss open to crack the vein that holds you, the final chapter that grew apart darkened the steps that parted my eyes. I wasn't meant to be warm, I wasn't meant to inhale the thoughts in your eyes. There are songs where I don't hear the music, I hear the footsteps of clouds filling the first tear with the weight of a year I couldn't smile, the versed sweater that never disclosed your spring complexion. Some things save you, some break you, and sometimes they're the same thing.

- rip tides

I don't think I've ever been home
until the first night you held me.
How was it so easy for me to fade from your fingerprints
when there's still evidence of your touch
all over my skin?
It's quite simple.
The love was here
and then it was not.
One second, I was yours
and the next I was on the floor
and I could smell my flesh burning.

- homesick

I had a dream
that you visited me.
You forced yourself down my throat
until I had no choice
but to swallow you
whole.
I woke up
and couldn't get the
metallic numbness
out of my mouth.
Our love was beautiful.
It could make paintings cry.
It was the kind of love
they write books about.
But when it ended,
and my world fell silent,
a sour bitterness filled my tongue
and now
I can never quite shake
the taste
of you.

- you're everywhere

I wasn't sure if it was going to be like last time,
when the circles were under my eyes
and you were laughing so hollow
that your bones rang with it.
But I need you to tell me what to do with my hands.
because when they aren't tangled in yours,
they are wrapped around my own throat.
I've been trying to learn the difference
between
writing poetry for you
and carving it into my skin
but these pages and ink
never quite bleed for you
the way my inner arms did
at 3am
after you left
and took my soul with you.
I wish there was a way
to summon the sun rays
a little bit earlier,
to give direction
to an infinite sea of thoughts.
I've found my fire
but only after years
spent pinning
for suns and stars
or getting lost in a galaxy
that was never really built
for the two of us.
You are the emptiness
of a crowded room.
You are every season when it is not.
You are the personification
of every ironic nightmare.
I stay up at night

clawing at my own skin
trying to get back
to where I was
before
you.

- depression

I've never been good at expressing my feelings. Sometimes I can't even find the right words to transpose my thoughts onto paper, but I never had a problem giving my soul, in its' rarest form to you.

- raw

Sometimes I stay up at night
waiting for your arms
to reach out from under the sheets
and wrap themselves around me. Sometimes I roll over in my
sleep
ready to curl up next to your warmth only to find the corpse of
our love. Sometimes I fill that void
with a new body
just to keep me sane
on sleepless nights,
but I'm always left
feeling homesick;
feigning for a pair of arms
that don't want to hold me.

- nostalgia

I saw stars in your eyes and tasted galaxies on your lips. I thought I could live forever in your sun rays.

- beautiful liar

I think of you more often than not.
How are you?
I hope you got that new job you wanted.
How's your mother?
I hope she still kisses you
every morning
and tells you she loves you
every night.
I hope your heart
never experiences
the end of the world
the way mine did
six months ago
when you decided
I no longer felt like
home.

- abandoned

They say the moment you fall down
is the moment you lose control of yourself.
Blue thoughts fading away
until the chroma of your being vanishes
behind the cerulean hues.
A fresh pair of eyes are watching you.
Waiting on your next move.
You are prey.
Vulnerable.
A victim to the isolation.
In this exile there is a soft-spoken aeration,
a bitter breath that permeates the flesh, raising hair and
whatever else is hidden.
To become a better you,
look no further than within.
Anxiety is the root to this fear.
Don't quit,
get up.
That ache for an unrequited prosperity
will leave your mouth bleeding
and your skin on fire.
The only way to distance yourself
from them
is if you
split.
Life's commitment
to self-examination
is a burden.
It can break you;
put your soul in handcuffs
and march it into the sunset.
Seek freedom
and become captive to your desires.
Seek discipline
and find your liberty.

You're brave,
strong,
and confident
Trace your vision until you find a path.
Resurrect;
and fight for what you want.
Your mind is blinded by the emptiness
of what used to be,
ghost lights throbbing,
haunting.
In the gaps, the dark spaces
between the bones and cosmic cracks,
there is a light.
Because you don't need wings
to fly in dreams.

-the lost soul feat. irvine b. paye

I fall in love so easily.
Maybe that's why I built these walls massive and secure
with trenches so deep,
maybe that's why I was hesitant
to let you in.
Because;
The first time
I met the ocean,
he waved to me
then pulled me in
ankles first
heart second.
The first time
I met the moon,
I mean the first time
I really saw it glistening in the sky
and kissing the stars
I fell for him too.
The first time
I met the mountain tops
with their vast glorious peaks,
they captured me like nothing else
and I felt myself
entertaining a new passion
for their immense beauty.

I thought all that was enough.
I didn't think I needed more.
 But then,
I met you.

And the first time
I met you,
your deep ocean eyes
wrapped me up like high tide.

Your crescent-shaped smile
created this instant demand
for your lips.
And when you did
kiss me
they brought me to heights
mountains couldn't touch.
The first time I met you,
I saw myself
falling again
for the last time.

- the last time

I cry for you most nights.

Not because I am sad,
but because my heart bleeds
for you;
for your happiness.
I crave it
more than my own.

I pray for your peace of mind — your well-being.

Do you pray for me?

I used to thank God for you.
I used to beg Him never to take you because I knew
I did not deserve you.

I used to curse God because of you.
I hated Him for proving
to me,
to us,
that I was unworthy.

I often let my mind wander
and replay those Sunday mornings spent wrapped in sheets
covered in sweetness
the air
smelled
like love.

I miss the warmth of your breath,
the hazel in your eyes
when the sunlight
peeked through the window.

I miss the way
 you wrapped your hands

around my scars
or tangled your fingertips
in mine.

I know you can't hold me anymore.
I know you kissed me when you
had to
not because
you wanted to.

I know you had sadness in your soul.

- pray

The darkness feels closer than ever
and sometimes
I let the weight sit a little longer
because I like the way
my chest stings
as my lungs
gasp
for air.

- choke

My body craves yours as if you were the last drop of water and I haven't had a decent drink in years.

- thirst

Self-harm seems a lot more poetic
when squeezed between words like
"romantic" and "aesthetic."
But there is nothing
beautiful
about this emptiness inside me
that's lingered long after
you've left.
I've tried to drown my pain
with sober thoughts
and spend nights
basking in the rays
of the early dawn.
You didn't make me.
You don't define me.
So, I don't know why
I cling to the image of us
wrapped in my sheets
on a Sunday afternoon.
The truth is
you made me
want me.
You made me love you
so much
that I forgot
how to
hate myself.
You promised me a forever
that was more breathtaking
than Adam and Eve's garden.
You had me daydreaming
about a future
that didn't exist outside
of the doctor-recommended
7 to 8 hours.

I have so many thoughts
in my head,
each one involving your skin
on mine.
But I can't seem to find the words
to describe the smell
of the burning flesh
where your hands used to hold me,
And how the pain
still feels better
than nothing.

-mutilation

I think I forgot what it felt like to fall asleep at night the moment you decided my body no longer felt like home. And I know I shouldn't let the opinions of those who have never known passion determine myself worth, but my smile has refused to blossom since that spring when the acid poured from your lips and drenched my garden. I'm beginning to learn how to love myself, and no longer in that self-pity kind of love. Like in the way you love the stray cats that come begging at your back door, or in the way you love receiving re-gifted items because it's "the thought that counts." I've realized I lit myself on fire just to keep you warm. I ripped my own heart out just to prove that it could still beat for you. All while you slit my throat, dangled band-aids above my head and held me while I bled into our arms, so you could show me that you're all I'd ever really need.

It wasn't me who needed saving.
It was you who needed me.

-a page from my diary // ego boost

I bought new furniture. I redecorated my bedroom. I bought new sheets, new paint for my walls, and a new life where your scent has not made home.

-rebirth

The words crawl out of your mouth and attach themselves to my skin. They bury themselves into my flesh until they are swimming through my veins-absorbing my blood stream and lighting my soul on fire. I opened up, allowing your flames to engulf me. Your words-embodying the beauty that no longer exists. Allowing my mind to caress a fabricated world solely formed out of your own spite. Your words- permitting me to fall in love with not so much what you say, but with how your mouth forms the "L" in love or the way your eyes sparkle as you puncture my heart.

-the sweetest lies

NADIA STARBINSKI